jam

jams, jellies & pickles

THE AUSTRALIAN
Women's Weekly

contents

AUSTRALIAN CUP AND SPOON MEASUREMENTS ARE METRIC. A CONVERSION CHART APPEARS ON PAGE 77.

Everyone loves homemade jam. It's a hundred times better than the kind you buy at the supermarket. Along with popular jellies and jams, there are recipes here for marmalades, relishes, pickles and chutneys. Have a go at making a preserve - they make beautiful gifts and are great for school fetes and market stalls.

Pamela Clark

Food Director

3

before you begin

EQUIPMENT

Choose a pan made from heavy aluminium, enamel or stainless steel; don't use copper or unsealed cast-iron pans, as the natural acids in fruit and vegetables will damage the surfaces of these pans, spoiling the flavour of the preserve.

As a guide to the size of saucepan to use, the preserve mixture should not be more than 5cm (2 inches) deep after all the ingredients have been added to the pan.

Most preserve recipes have a stage where they are cooked covered; the lid should be tight-fitting, as this is the stage where evaporation is not wanted.

STERILISING JARS

Here are three methods for sterilising jars. Start with cleaned washed jars and lids.

1 Put the jars and lids through the hottest cycle of a dishwasher without detergent.

2 Lie jars down in a boiler with lids, cover them with cold water then cover the boiler with a lid. Bring the water to the boil over a high heat and boil the jars for 20 minutes.

3 Stand jars upright, without touching each other, on a wooden board on the lowest shelf in the oven, place lids in too. Turn oven to the lowest possible temperature, close the oven door and leave the jars to heat through for 30 minutes.

Next, remove jars and lids from the oven or dishwasher with a towel, or from the boiling water with tongs and rubber-gloved hands; water will evaporate from hot wet jars quite quickly. Stand jars upright and not touching each other on a wooden board, or bench covered with a tea towel.

DO

Choose the best quality fresh-picked fruit (slightly under-ripe is best) or vegetables. Damaged or bruised fruit can result in mouldy preserves.

Stand marmalades, and some jams and conserves, after cooking to allow the pieces of fruit to settle and disperse through the syrup before bottling. The fruit can rise to the top of the jar if the jam is bottled too soon.

Be fussy about sterilising jars and lids. The jars should be hot when the hot preserve is poured into them.

Fill jars to the top with preserve; it will shrink slightly on cooling, leaving a small space between the lid and top surface of the preserve. Seal jars while hot.

Make small amounts of jam at a time. Colour, flavour and clarity will be better.

DON'T

Increase the quantities of preserve recipes unless you have the right large equipment. During cooking, about half the liquid evaporates; a wide-topped boiler is ideal for making most preserves.

Reduce the sugar content. Sugar is a preservative; preserves made without enough sugar will not keep.

Use jars that are cracked or chipped. Cracked jars will break when hot preserves are poured into them, and chips can harbour bacteria.

helpful steps

muslin bag
Tying various spices in a piece of muslin makes them easier to remove when the chutney (or other preserve) is ready to be poured into jars.

jelling
Dip a wooden spoon into the jam, and hold the bowl of the spoon towards you. If the jam is ready, two or three large drops will roll along the edge of the spoon to form almost a triangle of thick jam.

jelling
Drop a teaspoon of jam onto a chilled (from the fridge or freezer) saucer. The jam should cool quickly to room temperature.

jelling

Push the jam with your finger, the skin will wrinkle if the jam is ready. If the jam is not jelling, return it to the heat and boil it again.

jellies

Secure the cloth (unbleached calico or muslin) to the legs of an upturned stool. The cloth should sag, so that the heavy fruit mixture drips into a bowl below. Strain the fruit mixture through a damp cloth.

marmalade

Using a large metal spoon, remove and discard any scum from the surface of the marmalade.

jams, marmalades & jellies

ANY BERRY JAM

prep + cook time 40 minutes **makes** 4 cups
nutritional count per tablespoon 0g total fat (0g saturated fat);
326kJ (78 cal); 19.5g carbohydrate; 0.3g protein; 0.7g fibre

125g (4 ounces) blackberries
125g (4 ounces) blueberries
250g (8 ounces) raspberries
500g (1 pound) strawberries, hulled
⅓ cup (80ml) lemon juice
4 cups (880g) white (granulated) sugar

1 Stir ingredients in large saucepan over high heat, without boiling, until sugar dissolves; bring to the boil. Reduce heat; simmer, uncovered, without stirring, about 30 minutes or until jam jells when tested.
2 Pour hot jam into hot sterilised jars; seal immediately. Label and date jars when cold.
tip Use any combination of berries you like to collectively weigh 1kg (2 pounds).

APRICOT AND VANILLA BEAN JAM

prep + cook time 55 minutes **makes** 4 cups
nutritional count per tablespoon 0g total fat (0g saturated fat);
694kJ (166 cal); 43g carbohydrate; 0.1g protein; 0.4g fibre

1kg (2 pounds) fresh apricots,
   halved, seeded
1 vanilla bean, halved lengthways
1 cup (250ml) water
1kg (2 pounds) white (granulated) sugar

1 Combine apricots, vanilla bean and
the water in large saucepan; bring to the
boil. Reduce heat; simmer, covered, about
15 minutes or until mixture is pulpy.
2 Add sugar to pan; stir over high heat,
without boiling, until sugar dissolves.
Bring to the boil; boil, uncovered, without
stirring, about 35 minutes or until jam jells
when tested.
3 Discard vanilla bean. Pour hot jam into
hot sterilised jars; seal immediately. Label
and date jars when cold.

SPICED PLUM AND PORT JAM

prep + cook time 55 minutes **makes** 4 cups
nutritional count per tablespoon 0g total fat (0g saturated fat);
414kJ (99 cal); 24.6g carbohydrate; 0.1g protein; 0.4g fibre

1kg (2 pounds) plums, seeded, quartered
¼ cup (60ml) orange juice
1 cup (250ml) water
1 cinnamon stick, halved
½ teaspoon cloves
1 star anise
5 cups (1.1kg) white (granulated) sugar,
    approximately
½ cup (125ml) port

1 Combine plums, juice and the water in large saucepan; bring to the boil. Reduce heat; simmer, uncovered, about 15 minutes or until plums are pulpy.

2 Meanwhile, tie cinnamon, cloves and star anise in muslin.

3 Measure fruit mixture, allow 1 cup sugar for each cup of fruit mixture. Return fruit mixture, sugar, port and muslin bag to pan; stir over high heat, without boiling, until sugar dissolves. Bring to the boil; boil, uncovered, without stirring, about 35 minutes or until jam jells when tested.

4 Discard muslin bag. Pour hot jam into hot sterilised jars; seal immediately. Label and date jars when cold.

NO-COOK MIXED BERRY JAM

prep + cook time 20 minutes (+ standing) **makes** 7 cups
nutritional count per tablespoon 0.03g total fat (0.006g saturated fat);
191kJ (46 cal); 11.3g carbohydrate; 0.2g protein; 0.5g fibre

1kg (2 pounds) frozen mixed berries,
   thawed slightly
4 cups (880g) caster (superfine) sugar
½ cup (125ml) lemon juice

1 Crush berries lightly with a fork in large bowl; stir in sugar and juice. Cover, stand at room temperature for 24 to 36 hours, stirring occasionally to dissolve the sugar, until jam starts to set slightly.
2 Transfer jam to small freezer-proof containers; freeze until firm.
tips Use jam directly from freezer (just spoon out what you need – the amount of sugar means the jam never freezes solid) and immediately return the remaining jam to the freezer. If jam is defrosted it must be kept refrigerated and used within 3 days. No-cook jam can be frozen for up to 6 months. You can use any combination of frozen berries you like.

MULBERRY JAM

prep + cook time 30 minutes **makes** 3½ cups
nutritional count per tablespoon 0.05g total fat (0.02g saturated fat);
330kJ (79 cal); 19.5g carbohydrate; 0.5g protein; 0.6g fibre

1kg (2 pounds) mulberries
3½ cups (770g) white (granulated) sugar
¼ cup (60ml) water
1 tablespoon finely grated lemon rind
2 tablespoons lemon juice
1½ tablespoons powdered pectin (jamsetta)

1 Combine berries, sugar, the water, rind and juice in large saucepan; stir over high heat, without boiling, until sugar dissolves. Bring to the boil; boil, uncovered, without stirring, about 10 minutes or until berries are soft.

2 Carefully pour berry mixture into large heatproof jug; push about half the mixture through a fine sieve back into pan, discard seeds. Pour remaining berry mixture back into pan. Sprinkle pectin over jelly; boil, uncovered, about 5 minutes or until jam jells when tested.

3 Pour hot jam into hot sterilised jars; seal immediately. Label and date jars when cold.

CHERRY JAM

prep + cook time 1 hour **makes** 4 cups
nutritional count per tablespoon 0g total fat (0g saturated fat);
347kJ (83 cal); 21.2g carbohydrate; 0.2g protein; 0.4g fibre

1kg (2 pounds) cherries, halved, seeded
2 medium pears (460g), peeled, cored,
    chopped finely
⅓ cup (80ml) lemon juice
1 cup (250ml) water
4 cups (880g) white (granulated) sugar,
    approximately

1 Combine cherries, pear, juice and the water in large saucepan; bring to the boil. Reduce heat; simmer, covered, about 15 minutes or until cherries are soft.
2 Measure fruit mixture; allow 1 cup sugar for each cup of fruit mixture. Return fruit mixture and sugar to pan; stir over high heat, without boiling, until sugar dissolves. Bring to the boil; boil, uncovered, without stirring, about 30 minutes or until jam jells when tested.
3 Pour hot jam into hot sterilised jars; seal immediately. Label and date jars when cold.

BLUEBERRY AND APPLE JAM

prep + cook time 35 minutes **makes** 5 cups
nutritional count per tablespoon 0g total fat (0g saturated fat);
284kJ (68 cal); 17.2g carbohydrate; 0.1g protein; 0.4g fibre

1kg (2 pounds) blueberries
3 medium green-skinned apples (450g),
   peeled, cored, chopped finely
2 tablespoons lemon juice
4 cups (880g) white (granulated) sugar

1 Combine berries, apple and juice in large saucepan; bring to the boil. Reduce heat; simmer, uncovered, about 15 minutes or until berries are soft.
2 Add sugar to pan; stir over high heat, without boiling, until sugar dissolves. Bring to the boil; boil, uncovered, without stirring, about 20 minutes or until jam jells when tested.
3 Pour hot jam into hot sterilised jars; seal immediately. Label and date jars when cold.
tip Granny Smith apples are best for this recipe.

PEACH, RASPBERRY AND CHAMPAGNE JAM

prep + cook time 35 minutes **makes** 3 cups
nutritional count per tablespoon 0.06g total fat (0.01g saturated fat);
178kJ (43 cal); 9.5g carbohydrate; 0.3g protein; 1g fibre

500g (1 pound) peaches, peeled, seeded,
    chopped finely
500g (1 pound) raspberries
1½ cups (330g) white (granulated) sugar
1 tablespoon lemon juice
½ cup (125ml) pink champagne

1 Combine peaches, berries, sugar, juice
and half the champagne in large saucepan;
stir over high heat, without boiling, until
sugar dissolves. Bring to the boil; boil,
uncovered, without stirring, about
15 minutes or until jam jells when tested.
Stir in remaining champagne.
2 Pour hot jam into hot sterilised jars; seal
immediately. Label and date jars when cold.

PEACH AND PASSIONFRUIT JAM

prep + cook time 50 minutes **makes** 3 cups
nutritional count per tablespoon 0.4g total fat (0g saturated fat);
239kJ (57 cal); 14g carbohydrate; 0.3g protein; 0.6g fibre

1kg (2 pounds) peaches, peeled, seeded, chopped finely
½ cup (125ml) lemon juice
2 cups (440g) white (granulated) sugar, approximately
⅓ cup (80ml) passionfruit pulp

1 Combine peaches and juice in large saucepan; bring to the boil. Reduce heat; simmer, covered, about 15 minutes or until peaches are soft.
2 Measure fruit mixture; allow ¾ cup sugar for each cup of fruit mixture. Return fruit mixture and sugar to pan; stir over high heat, without boiling, until sugar dissolves. Bring to the boil; boil, uncovered, without stirring, about 15 minutes or until jam jells when tested. Stir in passionfruit.
3 Pour hot jam into hot sterilised jars; seal immediately. Label and date jars when cold.

RHUBARB AND GINGER JAM

prep + cook time 2 hours **makes** 6 cups
nutritional count per tablespoon 0g total fat (0g saturated fat);
259kJ (62 cal); 15.3g carbohydrate; 0.3g protein; 0.5g fibre

1.5kg (3 pounds) trimmed rhubarb,
   chopped coarsely
1 cup (250ml) water
2 tablespoons lemon juice
7cm (3-inch) piece fresh ginger (35g), grated
4½ cups (1kg) white (granulated) sugar,
   approximately
½ cup (90g) finely chopped glacé ginger

1 Combine rhubarb, the water, juice and fresh ginger in large saucepan; bring to the boil. Reduce heat; simmer, covered, about 30 minutes or until mixture is pulpy.
2 Measure fruit mixture, allow ¾ cup sugar for each cup of fruit mixture. Return fruit mixture, sugar and glacé ginger to pan; stir over high heat, without boiling, until sugar dissolves. Bring to the boil; boil, uncovered, without stirring, about 30 minutes or until jam jells when tested.
3 Pour hot jam into hot sterilised jars; seal immediately. Label and date jars when cold.
tip The rhubarb needs to be a deep red colour for this jam; under-ripe or green rhubarb will make the jam too tart in flavour.

RASPBERRY AND MINT JAM

prep + cook time 30 minutes **makes** 5 cups
nutritional count per tablespoon 0.1g total fat (0g saturated fat);
301kJ (72 cal); 17.7g carbohydrate; 0.2g protein; 1g fibre

6 sprigs fresh mint, chopped coarsely
1kg (2 pounds) raspberries
2 tablespoons lemon juice
1kg (2 pounds) white (granulated) sugar

1 Tie mint in muslin. Combine berries, muslin bag and juice in large saucepan; cook over low heat, stirring occasionally, about 5 minutes or until berries are soft.
2 Add sugar; stir over high heat, without boiling, until sugar dissolves. Bring to the boil; boil, uncovered, without stirring, about 15 minutes or until jam jells when tested.
3 Discard muslin bag. Pour hot jam into hot sterilised jars; seal immediately. Label and date jars when cold.

SPICED QUINCE AND PEAR JAM

prep + cook time 2 hours **makes** 8 cups
nutritional count per tablespoon 0.03g total fat (0g saturated fat);
256kJ (61 cal); 15.4g carbohydrate; 0.07g protein; 0.7g fibre

3 medium quinces (1kg), peeled, cored
3 large pears (990g), peeled, cored
5cm (2-inch) piece fresh ginger (25g),
    sliced thinly
2 star anise
1.5 litres (6 cups) water
⅔ cup (160ml) lemon juice
6 cups (1.3kg) white (granulated) sugar

1 Finely chop quince and pear. Tie ginger and star anise in muslin.
2 Combine fruit, muslin bag, the water and juice in large saucepan; bring to the boil. Reduce heat; simmer, covered, about 1 hour or until mixture is pulpy. Discard muslin bag.
3 Add sugar; stir over high heat, without boiling, until sugar dissolves. Bring to the boil; boil, uncovered, without stirring, about 30 minutes or until jam jells when tested.
4 Pour hot jam into hot sterilised jars; seal immediately. Label and date jars when cold.

MANGO, PASSIONFRUIT AND LIME JAM

prep + cook time 50 minutes **makes** 5 cups
nutritional count per tablespoon 0.06g total fat (0g saturated fat);
241kJ (58 cal); 14.1g carbohydrate; 0.3g protein; 0.6g fibre

2kg (4 pounds) mangoes, peeled, seeded,
   chopped finely
½ cup (125ml) lime juice
3 cups (660g) white (granulated) sugar,
   approximately
⅓ cup (80ml) passionfruit pulp
2 tablespoons finely grated lime rind

1 Combine mango and juice in large
saucepan; bring to the boil. Reduce heat;
simmer, covered, about 20 minutes or until
mango is soft.
2 Measure fruit mixture; allow ¾ cup sugar
for each cup of fruit mixture. Return fruit
mixture and sugar to pan; stir over high
heat, without boiling, until sugar dissolves.
Bring to the boil; boil, uncovered, without
stirring, about 15 minutes or until jam jells
when tested. Stir in passionfruit pulp and rind.
3 Pour hot jam into hot sterilised jars; seal
immediately. Label and date jars when cold.

CHUNKY FIG AND VANILLA JAM

prep + cook time 1 hour **makes** 3 cups
nutritional count per tablespoon 0.1g total fat (0g saturated fat);
351kJ (84 cal); 20.9g carbohydrate; 0.4g protein; 0.7g fibre

1kg (2 pounds) fresh whole figs
½ cup (125ml) orange juice
2 tablespoons lemon juice
1 vanilla bean, halved lengthways
3 cups (660g) white (granulated) sugar

1 Cut each unpeeled fig into eight wedges. Combine figs, juices and vanilla bean in large saucepan; bring to the boil. Reduce heat; simmer, covered, about 20 minutes or until figs are soft.
2 Add sugar to pan; stir over high heat, without boiling, until sugar dissolves. Bring to the boil; boil, uncovered, without stirring, about 30 minutes or until jam jells when tested. Discard vanilla bean.
3 Pour hot jam into hot sterilised jars; seal immediately. Label and date jars when cold.
tips You can use any variety of fresh fig for this recipe. Omit the vanilla bean for a plain fig jam.

GREEN TOMATO JAM

prep + cook time 1 hour 10 minutes **makes** 3½ cups
nutritional count per tablespoon 0g total fat (0g saturated fat);
238kJ (57 cal); 14.4g carbohydrate; 0.2g protein; 0.3g fibre

500g (1 pound) green-skinned apples,
   peeled, cored, chopped coarsely
4 medium green tomatoes (600g),
   chopped coarsely
1 teaspoon ground ginger
1 cinnamon stick
1 cup (250ml) water
2½ cups (550g) white (granulated) sugar,
   approximately

1 Combine apple, tomato, ginger, cinnamon and the water in large saucepan; bring to the boil. Reduce heat; simmer, covered, about 20 minutes or until fruit is soft. Discard cinnamon.
2 Measure fruit mixture, allow 1 cup sugar for each cup of fruit mixture. Return fruit mixture and sugar to pan; stir over high heat, without boiling, until sugar dissolves. Bring to the boil; boil, uncovered, without stirring, about 15 minutes or until jam jells when tested.
3 Pour hot jam into hot sterilised jars; seal immediately. Label and date jars when cold.
tip Granny Smith apples are best for this recipe.

SEVILLE ORANGE MARMALADE

prep + cook time 1 hour 50 minutes (+ standing) **makes** 10 cups
nutritional count per tablespoon 0g total fat (0g saturated fat);
280kJ (67 cal); 17.3g carbohydrate; 0.1g protein; 0.2g fibre

1kg (2 pounds) seville oranges
2 litres (8 cups) water
2kg (4 pounds) white (granulated) sugar,
   approximately

1 Slice oranges thinly, reserve seeds. Combine orange slices and the water in large saucepan; stand, covered, overnight. Place reserved seeds in small jug, barely cover with water; stand, covered, overnight.
2 Bring orange mixture to the boil. Reduce heat; simmer, covered, about 1 hour or until rind is soft.
3 Meanwhile, strain seeds, reserve liquid; discard seeds.
4 Measure orange mixture, allow 1 cup sugar for each cup of orange mixture. Return orange mixture, sugar and reserved seed liquid to pan; stir over high heat, without boiling, until sugar dissolves. Bring to the boil; boil, uncovered, without stirring, about 30 minutes or until marmalade jells when tested.
5 Pour hot marmalade into hot sterilised jars; seal immediately. Label and date jars when cold.

MASTER ORANGE MARMALADE

prep + cook time 1 hour 50 minutes **makes** 4 cups
nutritional count per tablespoon 0g total fat (0g saturated fat);
368kJ (88 cal); 22.5g carbohydrate; 0.2g protein; 0.4g fibre

1kg (2 pounds) oranges
1.5 litres (6 cups) water
4½ cups (1kg) white (granulated) sugar,
   approximately

1 Peel oranges, removing rind and white pith separately; slice rind thinly, reserve half the pith. Quarter oranges; slice flesh thinly, reserve any seeds. Tie reserved pith and seeds in muslin.
2 Combine rind, flesh, muslin bag and the water in large saucepan; bring to the boil. Reduce heat; simmer, covered, about 1 hour or until rind is soft. Discard muslin bag.

3 Measure fruit mixture, allow 1 cup sugar for each cup of fruit mixture. Return orange mixture and sugar to pan; stir over high heat, without boiling, until sugar dissolves. Bring to the boil; boil, uncovered, without stirring, about 30 minutes or until marmalade jells when tested.
4 Pour hot marmalade into hot sterilised jars; seal immediately. Label and date jars when cold.
tip This basic method of making marmalade will work with most citrus fruits including lemons, limes, grapefruit, pomelos and tangerines or various combinations of these fruits.

CUMQUAT MARMALADE

prep + cook time 1 hour 30 minutes (+ standing) **makes** 6 cups
nutritional count per tablespoon 0g total fat (0g saturated fat);
314kJ (75 cal); 19.2g carbohydrate; 0.1g protein; 0.3g fibre

1kg (2 pounds) cumquats
2 tablespoons lemon juice
1.25 litres (5 cups) water
6 cups (1.3kg) white (granulated) sugar

1 Quarter cumquats, being careful not to cut all the way through. Squeeze cumquats to release seeds. Tie seeds in muslin. Process cumquats until finely chopped. Combine cumquats, muslin bag, juice and the water in large saucepan; stand, covered, overnight.

2 Bring cumquat mixture to the boil. Reduce heat; simmer, covered, about 30 minutes or until rind is soft. Discard muslin bag.

3 Add sugar; stir over high heat, without boiling, until sugar dissolves. Bring to the boil; boil, uncovered, without stirring, about 30 minutes or until marmalade jells when tested.

4 Pour hot marmalade into hot sterilised jars; seal immediately. Label and date jars when cold.

tip A cumquat (kumquat) is a fruit that resembles a miniature orange, although it is not a citrus fruit. Is oval and oblong or round, and ranges from golden yellow to reddish-orange in colour when ripe. Has a thin, sweet skin with a tart, sour flesh.

MINT JELLY

prep + cook time 2 hours (+ standing) **makes** 6 cups
nutritional count per tablespoon 0g total fat (0g saturated fat);
288kJ (69 cal); 17.9g carbohydrate; 0.1g protein; 0.2g fibre

1kg (2 pounds) green-skinned apples,
   unpeeled, chopped coarsely
1.5 litres (6 cups) water
5½ cups (1.2kg) white (granulated) sugar,
   approximately
green food colouring
1 cup firmly packed fresh mint leaves

1 Combine apple and the water in large
saucepan; bring to the boil. Reduce heat;
simmer, covered, about 1 hour or until apple
is pulpy.
2 Strain mixture through a fine cloth into
large bowl. Stand 3 hours or overnight until
liquid stops dripping. Do not squeeze cloth;
discard pulp.
3 Measure apple liquid; allow 1 cup sugar
for each cup of liquid. Return apple liquid
and sugar to same pan; stir over high heat,
without boiling, until sugar dissolves. Bring
to the boil; boil rapidly, uncovered, without
stirring, about 30 minutes or until jelly jells
when tested.

4 Pour jelly into large heatproof jug; stir in
a little of the food colouring. Stand until jelly
is lukewarm (but not set).
5 Meanwhile, drop mint into small saucepan
of boiling water for 2 seconds; drain. Rinse
under cold water; drain, pat dry with
absorbent paper. Chop mint finely; stir into
lukewarm jelly.
6 Pour jelly into hot sterilised jars; seal
immediately. Label and date jars when cold.
tips Granny Smith apples are best for this
recipe. Store mint jelly in a cool, dark place
for 3 months. Refrigerate after opening.
The jelly has a natural soft pink colour before
the colouring is used; you can omit the
colouring, if you prefer.
serving suggestions Serve with roast
lamb, barbecued cutlets or chops.

CRANBERRY JELLY

prep + cook time 1 hour 20 minutes (+ standing) **makes** 4 cups
nutritional count per tablespoon 0.03g total fat (0g saturated fat);
351kJ (84 cal); 21.4g carbohydrate; 0.1g protein; 0.5g fibre

900g (1¾ pounds) fresh or frozen cranberries
500g (1 pound) green-skinned apples,
    unpeeled, chopped coarsely
1 tablespoon finely grated orange rind
1 litre (4 cups) water
4 cups (880g) white (granulated) sugar,
    approximately

1 Combine cranberries, apples, rind and the water in large saucepan; bring to the boil. Reduce heat; simmer, covered, about 30 minutes or until pulpy.
2 Strain mixture through a fine cloth into large bowl. Stand 3 hours or overnight until liquid stops dripping. Do not squeeze cloth; discard pulp.
3 Measure cranberry liquid; allow 1 cup sugar for each cup of liquid. Return cranberry liquid and sugar to pan; stir over high heat, without boiling, until sugar dissolves. Bring to the boil; boil rapidly, uncovered, without stirring, about 25 minutes or until jelly jells when tested.
4 Pour hot jelly into hot sterilised jars; seal immediately. Label and date jars when cold.
tip Granny Smith apples are best for this recipe.

QUINCE PASTE

prep + cook time 6 hours (+ cooling) **makes** 5 cups
nutritional count per tablespoon 0g total fat (0g saturated fat);
59kJ (14 cal); 17.3g carbohydrate; 0.1g protein; 1.3g fibre

6 medium quinces (2.1kg)
1½ cups (375ml) water
4 cups (880g) caster (superfine) sugar

1 Peel, quarter and core quinces; tie cores
in muslin. Coarsely chop quince flesh.
2 Combine quince flesh and muslin bag
with the water in large saucepan; bring to
the boil. Boil, covered, about 35 minutes or
until fruit is soft; discard muslin bag.
3 Strain fruit over large heatproof bowl,
reserving ½ cup of the liquid; cool
10 minutes. Blend or process fruit with the
reserved cooking liquid until smooth.
4 Return fruit mixture to pan with sugar;
cook, stirring, over low heat, until sugar
dissolves. Cook, over low heat, about
3½ hours, stirring frequently, until quince
paste is very thick and deep ruby coloured.

5 Meanwhile, preheat oven to 100°C/200°F.
Grease a loaf pan; line base with baking
paper, extending paper 5cm (2 inches) over
long sides.
6 Spread paste into pan. Bake about
1½ hours or until surface is dry to touch.
Cool paste in pan. Remove from pan; wrap
in baking paper, then in foil. Store in an
airtight container in the refrigerator.
tips When the paste is sufficiently cooked,
a wooden spoon drawn through the paste
will leave a very distinct trail across the
base of the saucepan. To dry out the paste,
you can also place it in a fan-forced oven
with only the fan working (no temperature
set) overnight.

serving suggestions Quince paste is a
great accompaniment to cheese, or can
be melted down and used in fruit tarts
and pies. It should be cut into small slices
to serve.

chutneys & pickles

BEETROOT CHUTNEY

prep + cook time 1¼ hours **makes** 6 cups
nutritional count per tablespoon 0g total fat (0g saturated fat);
96kJ (23 cal); 5.1g carbohydrate; 0.3g protein; 0.6g fibre

6 medium fresh beetroot (beets) (1kg),
   trimmed
2 teaspoons cumin seeds
1 cinnamon stick, broken
4 cardamom pods, bruised
4 large green-skinned apples (800g),
   peeled, cored, chopped coarsely
1 medium red onion (170g),
   chopped coarsely
2 cloves garlic, crushed
2cm (¾-inch) piece fresh ginger (10g), grated
1 cup (220g) white (granulated) sugar
2 cups (500ml) white vinegar
2 tablespoons lemon juice
1 teaspoon coarse cooking salt (kosher salt)

1 Boil, steam or microwave beetroot until tender; drain. When cool enough to handle, peel. Finely chop half the beetroot; blend or process remaining beetroot until smooth.
2 Tie spices in muslin. Combine pureed beetroot and muslin bag with apple, onion, garlic, ginger, sugar, vinegar, juice and salt in large saucepan; stir over high heat, without boiling, until sugar dissolves. Bring to the boil. Reduce heat; simmer, uncovered, stirring occasionally, 30 minutes. Add chopped beetroot; simmer, uncovered, about 10 minutes or until chutney is thick. Discard muslin bag.
3 Spoon hot chutney into hot sterilised jars; seal immediately. Label and date jars when cold.
tips Granny Smith apples are best for this recipe. Store chutney in a cool, dark place for at least 3 weeks before opening, then refrigerate. Wear disposable gloves when peeling beetroot as it can stain hands.

TOMATO AND SWEET CHILLI RELISH

prep + cook time 1 hour **makes** 3 cups
nutritional count per tablespoon 0.3g total fat (0.04g saturated fat);
82.4kJ (20 cal); 6.3g carbohydrate; 0.3g protein; 0.4g fibre

2 teaspoons olive oil
1 medium red onion (170g),
    chopped finely
800g (1½ pounds) ripe tomatoes,
    chopped coarsely
½ cup (125ml) sweet chilli sauce
½ cup (110g) white (granulated) sugar
¼ cup (60ml) red wine vinegar
2 teaspoons coarse cooking salt
    (kosher salt)

1 Heat oil in large saucepan; cook onion, stirring, until soft. Add remaining ingredients; cook, stirring, over high heat, without boiling, until sugar dissolves. Bring to the boil. Reduce heat; simmer, uncovered, stirring occasionally, about 40 minutes or until relish is thick.

2 Spoon hot relish into hot sterilised jars; seal immediately. Label and date jars when cold.

tips Relish will keep, refrigerated, for up to 3 weeks. Relish can be used straight away.
serving suggestions Serve with grilled meat, sausages, or on hamburgers and sandwiches.

GREEN TOMATO CHUTNEY

prep + cook time 2 hours **makes** 5 cups
nutritional count per tablespoon 0.1g total fat (0g saturated fat);
201kJ (48 cal); 10.8g carbohydrate; 0.5g protein; 0.8g fibre

2kg (4 pounds) green tomatoes, cored,
   chopped coarsely
2 large brown onions (400g),
   chopped coarsely
2 large green-skinned apples (400g),
   peeled, cored, chopped coarsely
2 cups (440g) raw sugar
2½ cups (625ml) cider vinegar
1 cup (150g) sultanas
4 fresh long red chillies, chopped finely
6 cloves garlic, chopped finely
2 teaspoons coarse cooking salt
   (kosher salt)

1 Stir ingredients in large saucepan over high heat, without boiling, until sugar dissolves; bring to the boil. Reduce heat; simmer, uncovered, stirring occasionally, about 1½ hours or until chutney is thick.
2 Spoon hot chutney into hot sterilised jars; seal immediately. Label and date jars when cold.

tips Granny Smith apples are best for this recipe. Store chutney in a cool, dark place for at least 3 weeks before opening. Refrigerate after opening. This recipe is quite spicy; for a milder version you can remove the seeds from the chillies or use less chilli.
serving suggestions Serve with cold meats and cheese or on sandwiches and burgers.

MANGO CHUTNEY

prep + cook time 1¼ hours **makes** 4 cups
nutritional count per tablespoon 0.1g total fat (0g saturated fat);
196kJ (47cal); 10.7g carbohydrate; 0.5g protein; 0.7g fibre

3 medium mangoes (1.3kg),
   chopped coarsely
1 cup (150g) coarsely chopped
   dried apricots
2 medium red onions (340g), chopped finely
1½ cups (330g) firmly packed
   light brown sugar
2 cups (500ml) cider vinegar
6 cloves garlic, chopped finely
1 teaspoon ground ginger
½ teaspoon dried chilli flakes
1 teaspoon coarse cooking salt (kosher salt)

1 Stir ingredients in large saucepan over high heat, without boiling, until sugar dissolves; bring to the boil. Reduce heat; simmer, uncovered, stirring occasionally, about 1 hour or until chutney is thick.
2 Spoon hot chutney into hot sterilised jars; seal immediately. Label and date jars when cold.
tip Store chutney in a cool, dark place for at least 3 weeks before opening. Refrigerate after opening.
serving suggestions Serve with grilled meats, fish or curries.

CHILLI JAM

prep + cook time 1¾ hours (+ cooling) **makes** 3⅓ cups
nutritional count per tablespoon 0g total fat (0g saturated fat);
226kJ (54 cal); 13.1g carbohydrate; 0.4g protein; 0.4g fibre

1kg (2 pounds) ripe egg (plum) tomatoes,
  chopped coarsely
2¼ cups (500g) caster (superfine) sugar
⅓ cup (80ml) white vinegar
¼ cup (60ml) lemon juice
6 fresh long red chillies, sliced thinly
2 fresh small red thai (serrano) chillies,
  sliced thinly
4cm (1½-inch) piece fresh ginger (20g), grated
3 cloves garlic, crushed
2 tablespoons fish sauce
1 teaspoon coarse cooking salt (kosher salt)

1 Stir ingredients in large saucepan over high heat, without boiling, until sugar dissolves. Bring to the boil. Reduce heat; simmer, uncovered, stirring occasionally, about 1¼ hours or until jam is thick. Cool 15 minutes.

2 Blend or process chilli mixture, in batches, until smooth. Pour into hot sterilised jars; seal immediately. Label and date jars when cold.

tips Store in a cool, dark place for up to 3 months. Refrigerate after opening. Wear plastic disposable gloves when cutting chillies as they can burn your skin.

serving suggestions Use in stir-fries, marinades and sauces; use sparingly, as it's very hot.

SWEET RED ONION CHUTNEY

prep + cook time 2 hours 30 minutes **makes** 5½ cups
nutritional count per tablespoon 0.6g total fat (0.09g saturated fat);
164kJ (39 cal); 7.7g carbohydrate; 0.5g protein; 0.6g fibre

2 tablespoons olive oil
2kg (4 pounds) red onions, chopped coarsely
2 dried bay leaves
10 black peppercorns, crushed
4 sprigs fresh thyme
2 cups (440g) firmly packed
   light brown sugar
2 cups (500ml) red wine vinegar
2 teaspoons coarse cooking salt
   (kosher salt)

1 Heat oil in large saucepan; cook onion, stirring, about 15 minutes or until softened.
2 Meanwhile, tie bay leaves, peppercorns and thyme in muslin. Add muslin bag and remaining ingredients to pan; stir over high heat, without boiling, until sugar dissolves. Bring to the boil. Reduce heat; simmer, uncovered, stirring occasionally, about 1¾ hours or until chutney is thick.
3 Spoon hot chutney into hot sterilised jars; seal immediately. Label and date jars when cold.

tip Store chutney in a cool, dark place for at least 3 weeks before opening. Refrigerate after opening.
serving suggestions Serve with hamburgers, sausages and barbecued meats or stir a little through sauces.

PICCALILLI

prep + cook time 30 minutes (+ standing) **makes** 10 cups
nutritional count per tablespoon 0g total fat (0g saturated fat);
59kJ (14 cal); 2.6g carbohydrate; 0.3g protein; 0.3g fibre

400g (12½ ounces) small pickling
    onions, peeled
½ cup (140g) coarse cooking salt
    (kosher salt)
2 cups (500ml) boiling water
1.75 litres (7 cups) cold water
1 small cauliflower (1kg),
    cut into small florets
250g (8 ounces) green beans,
    trimmed, chopped coarsely
2 medium carrots (240g),
    chopped coarsely
1 cup (220g) white (granulated) sugar
⅓ cup (50g) plain (all-purpose) flour
2 tablespoons mustard powder
2 teaspoons ground turmeric
½ teaspoon cayenne pepper
1 litre (4 cups) cider vinegar

1 Peel onions, leaving the roots intact to hold the onions together. Combine salt and the boiling water in large non-metallic heatproof bowl; stir until salt dissolves. Add the cold water. Add vegetables; mix well. Cover with a large plate, or snap-lock bag half-filled with water, to keep vegetables submerged; stand overnight.
2 Rinse and drain vegetables well; drain on absorbent paper.
3 Combine sugar, flour and spices in large saucepan; gradually whisk in vinegar until smooth. Cook, stirring, until mixture boils and thickens. Add vegetables; simmer, uncovered, about 10 minutes or until vegetables are barely tender.
4 Spoon hot piccalilli into hot sterilised jars; seal immediately. Label and date jars when cold.

tip Store piccalilli in a cool, dark place for at least 3 weeks before opening. Refrigerate after opening.

serving suggestion Serve as part of a ploughman's lunch – a cold lunch usually consisting of thick crusty bread, cold meats, cheese and pickles.

SWEET MUSTARD PICKLE

prep + cook time 45 minutes (+ standing) **makes** 9 cups
nutritional count per tablespoon 0g total fat (0g saturated fat);
84kJ (20 cal); 4.9g carbohydrate; 0.2g protein; 0.2g fibre

½ cup (140g) coarse cooking salt
(kosher salt)
2 cups (500ml) boiling water
1 litre (4 cups) cold water
500g (1 pound) cauliflower,
chopped coarsely
4 medium brown onions (600g),
chopped coarsely
2 lebanese cucumbers (260g), unpeeled,
chopped coarsely
3 cups (750ml) cider vinegar
2 cups (440g) white (granulated) sugar
1 tablespoon mustard powder
1 teaspoon curry powder
1 teaspoon turmeric
⅓ cup (50g) cornflour (cornstarch)
2 tablespoons water

1 Combine salt and the boiling water in large non-metallic bowl; stir until salt dissolves. Add the cold water. Add vegetables; mix well. Cover with a large plate, or snap-lock bag half-filled with water, to keep vegetables submerged; stand overnight.

2 Rinse and drain vegetables well; drain on absorbent paper.

3 Combine vegetables, vinegar, sugar and spices in large saucepan; stir over high heat, without boiling, until sugar dissolves. Bring to the boil. Reduce heat; simmer, uncovered, 10 minutes or until vegetables are tender.

4 Blend cornflour with the water in small jug until smooth, add to pan; cook, stirring, until mixture boils and thickens.

5 Spoon hot pickle into hot sterilised jars; seal immediately. Label and date jars when cold.

tip Store pickles in a cool, dark place for at least 3 weeks before opening. Refrigerate after opening.

serving suggestions Serve with cold meats, burgers and sausages or on ham sandwiches.

PRESERVED LEMONS

prep time 15 minutes **makes** 16 pieces
nutritional count per piece 0.1g total fat (0.1g saturated fat);
88kJ (21 cal); 1.8g carbohydrate; 0.4g protein; 1.6g fibre

8 medium lemons (1.1kg)
1½ cups (450g) rock salt
5 fresh bay leaves
1 teaspoon coriander seeds
1 teaspoon caraway seeds
1 cup (250ml) lemon juice

1 Halve lemons lengthways; carefully cut each lemon half in half again, without cutting all the way through. Open lemon halves out slightly.

2 Squeeze lemons over a large non-metallic bowl to catch the juice; add lemons to bowl with salt, bay leaves and seeds, mix well.

3 Pack lemon mixture into 1.5-litre (6-cup) sterilised jar; pour enough of the juice into the jar to cover lemons. Place a snap-lock bag filled with water on top of the lemons to keep them submerged; seal jar. Label and date jar.

tips Store preserved lemons in a cool, dark place for at least 3 weeks before using. Refrigerate after opening. To use, remove and discard pulp, squeeze juice from rind, rinse rind well, then slice according to the recipe. Cinnamon sticks or chillies can be added to the preserved lemons at step 2.

serving suggestions Use the rinsed preserved lemon rind in tagines, couscous, salads, sauces, stews and pilafs.

CRACKED OLIVES

prep time 1 hour 30 minutes (+ standing) **makes** about 25 cups (3kg) drained olives
nutritional count per ¼ cup 2.2g total fat (0.3g saturated fat);
88kJ (21 cal); 0.4g carbohydrate; 0.2g protein; 0.4g fibre

5kg (10 pounds) green olives
2 tablespoons coarse cooking salt
  (kosher salt)
2 cloves garlic, crushed
1 teaspoon dried chilli flakes
2 teaspoons dried mixed herbs
4 litres (16 cups) olive oil, approximately

1 Using a small hammer, or the flat side of a meat mallet, carefully crack, but do not seed, each olive on a kitchen board. Place olives in large non-metallic bowl, plastic tub or bucket; cover with cold water. Cover with a large plate or a sealed plastic bag filled with water to keep olives submerged. Stand 12 to 16 days, changing the water every day, until olives become dark and tender. Drain olives, but do not rinse.
2 Combine drained olives, salt, garlic, chilli and herbs in large strainer; stand in sink overnight.
3 Spoon olives into sterilised jars; pour in enough olive oil to cover olives. Label and date jars.

tips You must use fresh, raw green olives, not those from the deli, as these have already been brined. Green olives range from light green to a mottled dark olive green colour; these are all fine to use. Olives have a short season, and are usually available during autumn. Warn anyone eating these olives that they still contain the seed. Store in a cool, dark place for at least 2 weeks before opening. Olives will keep for up to 12 months; refrigerate after opening. The amount of olive oil you will need depends on the size and shape of the jars used. Pack olives tightly into the jar but be gentle to avoid bruising. Olives may float to the surface; to keep them submerged, place a slice of lemon or a sealed small plastic bag filled with water on top of the olives before closing the jars. You can change the flavourings of marinated olives to suit your taste. Try adding sprigs of thyme, rosemary or dried oregano, strips of lemon or orange rind, bay leaves, peppercorns, sun-dried tomatoes or mustard seeds.
serving suggestion Serve with antipasto.

PICKLED RED CABBAGE

prep + cook time 30 minutes (+ standing) **makes** 5 cups
nutritional count per tablespoon 0.07g total fat (0.02g saturated fat);
68kJ (16 cal); 2.5g carbohydrate; 0.5g protein; 0.7g fibre

1kg (2 pounds) red cabbage, sliced thinly
2 medium red onions (340g), sliced thinly
2 tablespoons coarse cooking salt
   (kosher salt)
1 litre (4 cups) white vinegar
½ cup (110g) raw sugar
1 cinnamon stick, crushed coarsely
8 cloves
1 teaspoon allspice berries (pimento)

1 Combine cabbage and onion in large non-metallic bowl; sprinkle with salt, mix well. Cover; stand overnight.
2 Rinse and drain cabbage mixture well; drain on absorbent paper. Pack into hot sterilised jars.
3 Stir remaining ingredients in medium saucepan over high heat, without boiling, until sugar dissolves. Bring to the boil; remove from heat. Strain vinegar mixture into medium heatproof jug; discard solids. Pour enough vinegar mixture into jars to cover cabbage mixture; seal immediately. Label and date jars when cold.

tips Store pickle in a cool, dark place for at least 3 weeks before opening. Refrigerate after opening. The cabbage will lose its colour on standing.
serving suggestions Serve with pork, ham or grilled steaks or sausages.

ONION JAM

prep + cook time 1 hour **makes** 2¼ cups
nutritional count per tablespoon 4.6g total fat (0.6g saturated fat);
426kJ (102 cal); 13.4g carbohydrate; 1.2g protein; 1.1g fibre

¼ cup (60ml) olive oil
1kg (2 pounds) brown onions, sliced thinly
1 sprig fresh rosemary
⅔ cup (160ml) balsamic vinegar
½ cup (110g) firmly packed light brown sugar

1 Heat oil in large saucepan; cook onion and rosemary, stirring occasionally, about 25 minutes or until onion is soft and browned lightly. Add vinegar; cook, stirring, about 5 minutes or until liquid is absorbed. Add sugar; cook, stirring, about 10 minutes or until onion is caramelised and jam is thick.
2 Spoon hot jam into hot sterilised jars; seal immediately. Label and date jars when cold.
tips Store onion jam in the refrigerator. Use a mandoline or V-slicer to slice onions as thinly as possible – it's much faster and easier than using a knife.
serving suggestions Serve on burgers and sandwiches, in quiches and tarts, or with barbecued meat.

ALLSPICE also called pimento or jamaican pepper, tastes like a combination of nutmeg, cumin, clove and cinnamon – all spices. Available in ground form, or as berries, from good spice shops.

BAY LEAF aromatic leaves from the bay tree. Available fresh and dried.

BUTTER use salted or unsalted (sweet) butter; 125g is equal to one stick (4 ounces) of butter.

unsalted butter simply has no added salt. It is mainly used when making citrus or passionfruit curd.

CARDAMOM available in pod, seed or ground form. It has a distinctive aromatic, sweetly rich flavour and is one of the world's most expensive spices.

CAYENNE PEPPER see chilli.

CHERRIES, GLACÉ cooked in a heavy sugar syrup then dried.

CHILLI available in many different types and sizes. Use rubber gloves when seeding and chopping fresh chillies as they can burn your skin. Generally, the smaller the chilli, the hotter it is.

cayenne pepper a long, thin-fleshed, extremely hot red chilli usually sold dried and ground.

dried flakes deep-red, dehydrated chilli slices and whole seeds.

kashmiri these do not necessarily come from Kashmir; they are a popular Indian chilli with a high colour content, making the food they are used in a bright red colour without adding too much heat.

long green any unripened chilli; also some particular varieties that are ripe when green, such as jalapeño, habanero, poblano or serrano.

long red available both fresh and dried; a generic term used for any moderately hot, long (about 6cm to 8cm), thin chilli.

powder the Asian variety, made from dried ground red thai chillies, is the hottest; substitute for fresh chillies in the proportion of ½ teaspoon ground chilli powder to 1 medium chopped fresh chilli.

red thai also called 'scuds'; small, very hot and bright red in colour.

CINNAMON dried inner bark of the shoots of the cinnamon tree; available in stick (quill) or ground form.

CITRIC ACID is commonly found in most fruits, especially limes and lemons. Commercial citric acid accentuates the acid flavour of fruit, however, it is not a preservative.

CLOVES dried flower buds of a tropical tree; can be used whole or in ground form. Has a distinctively pungent and 'spicy' scent and flavour.

CORIANDER also known as pak chee, cilantro or chinese parsley; bright-green leafy herb with a pungent flavour. Both the stems and roots of coriander are used in cooking; wash well before using.

CORNFLOUR (CORNSTARCH) used as a thickening agent. Available as 100% maize (corn) and wheaten cornflour.

CUCUMBER, LEBANESE short, slender and thin-skinned. Probably the most popular variety because of its tender, edible skin, tiny seeds and sweet, fresh taste.

CUMIN also known as zeera or comino; this tiny dried seed has a spicy, nutty flavour. Available in seed form or dried and ground.

CURRY POWDER a blend of ground spices consisting of dried coriander, chilli, cinnamon, cumin, fenugreek, fennel, mace, cardamom and turmeric. Available in mild and hot varieties.

DILL this herb develops fine feathery leaves from a single stalk. Sweet and slightly tangy in flavour, dill has the best flavour when used fresh but dried dill is also available.

FENUGREEK the leaves and seeds are available dried or ground; the seeds have a bitter taste. Often used in curries.

FIVE-SPICE POWDER (CHINESE FIVE-SPICE) a fragrant mixture of ground cinnamon, cloves, star anise, sichuan pepper and fennel seeds.

FLAT-LEAF PARSLEY also known as continental or italian parsley.

FLOUR, PLAIN an all-purpose flour made from wheat.

GARAM MASALA a blend of spices based on varying proportions of cloves, cardamom, cinnamon, fennel, cumin and coriander, roasted and ground together. Black pepper and chilli can be added for a hotter version.

GHERKIN a very small variety of pickled cucumber; when pickled with dill it is known as a dill pickle.

GINGER

glacé fresh ginger root preserved in sugar syrup. Crystallised ginger can be substituted if rinsed with warm water and dried before using.

ground also powdered ginger; cannot be substituted for fresh ginger.

HERBS, DRIED MIXED a blend of dried crushed thyme, rosemary, marjoram, basil, oregano and sage.

JAMSETTA a powdered pectin product that helps set jam.

MANDARIN a small, loose-skinned citrus fruit also known as tangerine.

GLOSSARY

MINT a herb that includes many varieties including spearmint, common mint and peppermint. Spearmint has long, smooth leaves, and is the one greengrocers sell, while common mint, with rounded, pebbly leaves, is the one that most people grow. Spearmint has the stronger flavour.

MIXED SPICE a blend of ground spices usually consisting of cinnamon, allspice and nutmeg.

MUSHROOMS, BUTTON small, cultivated white mushrooms with a delicate, subtle flavour.

MUSTARD

powder finely ground yellow (white) mustard seeds.

seeds yellow mustard seeds, also known as white mustard seeds, are ground and used for mustard powder and in most prepared mustards. Black are also known as brown mustard seeds; they are more pungent than the yellow variety and are used in curries. Available from major supermarkets.

NECTARINES a variety of peach; available with white or yellow flesh. Can be either clingstone (when cut, flesh clings to the stone) or freestone (when cut, flesh will fall or twist cleanly away from the stone).

NUTMEG the dried nut of an evergreen tree native to Indonesia; it is available in ground form or you can grate your own with a fine grater.

OIL

olive made from the first pressing of ripened olives. Extra virgin and virgin are the best, while extra light or light refers to taste, not fat levels.

vegetable any of a number of oils that have been sourced from plants rather than animal fats.

OLIVES

black have a richer and more mellow flavour than the green ones and are softer in texture. Sold either plain or in a piquant marinade.

green those harvested before fully ripened and are, as a rule, denser and more bitter than their black relatives.

kalamata small, sharp-tasting, brine-cured black olives.

niçoise small black olives.

pimento-stuffed a green olive with a lively, briny bitterness containing a morsel of capsicum (pepper), which adds a flash of colour.

OREGANO a herb, also known as wild marjoram; has a woody stalk with clumps of tiny, dark green leaves that have a pungent, peppery flavour and are used fresh or dried.

PAPRIKA ground dried sweet red capsicum (pepper); there are many types available, including sweet, hot, mild and smoked.

PATTY-PAN SQUASH also called crookneck or custard marrow pumpkin; a round, slightly flat, summer squash, yellow or pale-green in colour with a scalloped edge. Harvested young, it has a firm white flesh and a distinct flavour.

PEACHES come in yellow and white varieties, both of which can be either clingstone or freestone, defined by whether the flesh separates cleanly from the stone. See also nectarines.

PEPPERCORN MEDLEY this is a combination of black, white and green peppercorns; it is fine to just use the same amount of black peppercorns if you can't get the medley. Available from most major supermarkets.

PLUMS can be clingstone or freestone, defined by whether the flesh separates cleanly from the stone. *See also nectarines.*

PUMPKIN a large rounded or elongated thick-skinned fruit, which is usually orange or yellow, though may also be dark green; has an edible flesh beneath its thick skin, which contains many seeds. May also be known as gourd, squash or winter squash.

RAISINS dried sweet grapes.

RED CABBAGE is good raw in salads; otherwise, cook slowly and gently with a minimum of water plus an acid ingredient such as apple, vinegar or wine. The acid component is needed because plain water may be alkaline, which turns red cabbage a discouraging blue-green colour with a flavour to match.

ROSEMARY a woody, evergreen Mediterranean herb with strong, resinous fragrance and flavour.

SALT

coarse cooking is coarser than table salt, but not as large-flaked as sea salt. Sold in most supermarkets.

rock sold in large crystals, rock salt has a greyish hue because it is unrefined.

SAUCES

chilli bean a hot, spicy, salty sauce made from fermented broad beans, soya beans, rice, chillies and spices.

fish also called *nam pla* or *nuoc nam*; is made from pulverised salted fermented fish, most often anchovies. Has a pungent smell and strong taste; use sparingly.

soy also known as sieu, is made from fermented soya beans. Several variations are available in most supermarkets and Asian food stores.

dark soy is deep brown, almost black in colour; rich, with a thicker consistency than other types. Pungent but not particularly salty.

japanese soy an all-purpose low-sodium sauce made with more wheat content than its Chinese counterparts; fermented in barrels and aged.

light soy fairly thin in consistency and, while paler than the others, the saltiest tasting; used in dishes in which the natural colour of the ingredients is to be maintained. Don't confuse with salt-reduced or low-sodium soy sauces.

sweet chilli a mild, Thai sauce made with chillies, sugar, garlic and vinegar.

Tabasco brand name of an extremely fiery sauce made from vinegar, thai red chillies and salt.

worcestershire made from soy sauce, garlic, tamarind, onions, molasses, lime, anchovies, vinegar and other seasonings.

SUGAR

brown light brown is an extremely soft, finely granulated sugar retaining molasses for its characteristic colour and flavour.

caster also known as superfine or finely granulated table sugar.

dark brown moist with a rich, distinctive full flavour coming from natural molasses syrup.

palm sugar also known as nam tan pip, jaggery, jawa or gula melaka; made from the sap of the sugar palm tree. Light brown to black in colour and usually sold in rock-hard cakes. Substitute with brown sugar.

raw a natural brown granulated sugar. Gives a slight caramel flavour.

white a coarse, granulated table sugar, also known as crystal sugar.

SULTANAS dried grapes, also known as golden raisins.

SUMAC a purple-red, astringent spice ground from berries growing on shrubs that flourish wild around the Mediterranean; adds a tart, lemony flavour. Available from Middle-Eastern food stores and major supermarkets.

TANGELO a loose-skinned, juicy, sweetly-tart citrus fruit with few seeds.

TARRAGON an aromatic herb with dark green leaves and an anise-like flavour. Store stems down in a glass of water with a plastic bag on top. Known as the 'king of herbs' in France.

THYME a member of the mint family, it has tiny grey-green leaves that give off a pungent minty, light-lemon aroma. Fresh thyme should be stored in the refrigerator, wrapped in a damp paper towel and placed in a sealed bag for no more than a few days.

lemon thyme a herb with a lemony scent, which is due to the high level of citral in its leaves – an oil also found in lemon, orange, verbena and lemon grass. The citrus scent is enhanced by crushing the leaves in your hands before using the herb.

TOMATOES, SEMI-DRIED partially dried tomato pieces in olive oil; softer and juicier than sun-dried, these are not a preserve thus do not keep as long as sun-dried.

TREACLE a concentrated, refined sugar syrup with a distinctive flavour

and dark black colour; similar to molasses but is less bitter and viscous.

TURMERIC, GROUND a member of the ginger family, its root is dried and ground, resulting in the rich yellow powder that adds a characteristic golden colour to foods. It is intensely pungent in taste, but not hot.

VINEGAR

balsamic originally from Modena, Italy, there are now many balsamic vinegars on the market ranging in pungency and quality depending on how long they have been aged. Made from a regional wine of white Trebbiano grapes specially processed and aged in antique wooden casks to give the exquisite pungent flavour. It is a deep rich brown colour with a sweet and sour flavour. Quality can be determined up to a point by price; use the most expensive sparingly.

cider (apple cider) made from fermented apples.

malt (brown malt) is made from fermented malt and beech shavings.

red wine based on fermented red wine.

rice wine made from rice wine lees (sediment left after fermentation), salt and alcohol.

white made from spirit of cane sugar.

white wine made from a blend of white wines.

ZUCCHINI also called courgette; small, pale- or dark-green, yellow or white vegetable belonging to the squash family. Harvested when young, its edible flowers can be stuffed then deep-fried to make a delicious appetiser. The stem of the zucchini is the baby zucchini attached to the flower.

CONVERSION CHART

MEASURES

One Australian metric measuring cup holds approximately 250ml, one Australian metric tablespoon holds 20ml, one Australian metric teaspoon holds 5ml.

The difference between one country's measuring cups and another's is within a 2- or 3-teaspoon variance, and will not affect your cooking results. North America, New Zealand and the United Kingdom use a 15ml tablespoon. All cup and spoon measurements are level. The most accurate way of measuring dry ingredients is to weigh them. When measuring liquids, use a clear glass or plastic jug with metric markings.

We use large eggs with an average weight of 60g.

DRY MEASURES

METRIC	IMPERIAL
15g	½oz
30g	1oz
60g	2oz
90g	3oz
125g	4oz (¼lb)
155g	5oz
185g	6oz
220g	7oz
250g	8oz (½lb)
280g	9oz
315g	10oz
345g	11oz
375g	12oz (¾lb)
410g	13oz
440g	14oz
470g	15oz
500g	16oz (1lb)
750g	24oz (1½lb)
1kg	32oz (2lb)

LIQUID MEASURES

METRIC	IMPERIAL
30ml	1 fluid oz
60ml	2 fluid oz
100ml	3 fluid oz
125ml	4 fluid oz
150ml	5 fluid oz
190ml	6 fluid oz
250ml	8 fluid oz
300ml	10 fluid oz
500ml	16 fluid oz
600ml	20 fluid oz
1000ml (1 litre)	1¾ pints

LENGTH MEASURES

METRIC	IMPERIAL
3mm	⅛in
6mm	¼in
1cm	½in
2cm	¾in
2.5cm	1in
5cm	2in
6cm	2½in
8cm	3in
10cm	4in
13cm	5in
15cm	6in
18cm	7in
20cm	8in
23cm	9in
25cm	10in
28cm	11in
30cm	12in (1ft)

OVEN TEMPERATURES

These oven temperatures are only a guide for conventional ovens.
For fan-forced ovens, check the manufacturer's manual.

	°C (CELSIUS)	°F (FAHRENHEIT)
Very slow	120	250
Slow	150	275-300
Moderately slow	160	325
Moderate	180	350-375
Moderately hot	200	400
Hot	220	425-450
Very hot	240	475

The imperial measurements used in these recipes are approximate only. Measurements for cake pans are approximate only. Using same-shaped cake pans of a similar size should not affect the outcome of your baking. We measure the inside top of the cake pan to determine sizes.

INDEX

Published in 2012 by ACP Books, Sydney

ACP Books are published by ACP Magazines Limited,
a division of Nine Entertainment Co.

54 Park St, Sydney
GPO Box 4088, Sydney, NSW 2001.

phone (+61)2 9282 8618; fax (+61)2 9126 3702

acpbooks@acpmagazines.com.au; www.acpbooks.com.au

ACP Books

Publishing director, ACP Magazines - Gerry Reynolds

Publisher - Sally Wright

Editorial & food director - Pamela Clark

Creative director - Hieu Chi Nguyen

Sales & rights director - Brian Cearnes

Published and Distributed in the United Kingdom by Octopus Publishing Group

Endeavour House

189 Shaftesbury Avenue

London WC2H 8JY

United Kingdom

phone (+44)(0)207 632 5400; fax (+44)(0)207 632 5405

info@octopus-publishing.co.uk;

www.octopusbooks.co.uk

Printed by Toppan Printing Co, China

International foreign language rights - Brian Cearnes, ACP Books bcearnes@acpmagazines.com.au

A catalogue record for this book is available from the British Library.
ISBN 978-1-74245-282-1